TO THE EXTREME

Extreme Surfing

by Christine Peterson

Reading Consultant:
Barbara J. Fox
Reading Specialist
North Carolina State University

Capstone
press

Mankato, Minnesota

Blazers is published by Capstone Press,
151 Good Counsel Drive, P.O. Box 669, Mankato, Minnesota 56002.
www.capstonepub.com

Books published by Capstone Press are manufactured with paper
containing at least 10 percent post-consumer waste.

Library of Congress Cataloging-in-Publication Data
Peterson, Christine, 1961–
    Extreme surfing / By Christine Peterson.
    p. cm.—(Blazers—to the extreme)
    Includes bibliographical references and index.
    ISBN-13: 978-0-7368-3786-6 (hardcover)
    ISBN-10: 0-7368-3786-8 (hardcover)
    ISBN-13: 978-0-7368-5221-0 (softcover pbk.)
    ISBN-10: 0-7368-5221-2 (softcover pbk.)
    1. Surfing—Juvenile literature. I. Title. II. Series.
GV840.S8P44 2005
797.3'2—dc22   2004016036

Summary: Describes the sport of extreme surfing, including tricks
and safety information.

Credits
Jason Knudson, set designer; Enoch Peterson and Steve Christensen,
    book designers; Scott Thoms, photo editor; Kelly Garvin,
    photo researcher

Photo Credits
Darrell Wong, 5, 6, 7, 8
Getty Images Inc./Chris McGrath, 15, 27; Mr. Price Pro/Karen Wilson,
    cover; Pierre Tostee, 23
Surfpix/Gary Hill, 20; Phil Holden, 21; Sean Davey, 11, 12–13, 14,
    16–17, 19, 22, 25, 28–29

**Capstone Press thanks Paul West, president, United States Surfing
Federation, for his assistance with this book.**

Printed in the United States of America in Stevens Point, Wisconsin.
062011
006228WZVMI

Table of Contents

Surfing Jaws

A monster wave rises out of the ocean near Hawaii. It curls around a surfer as if to swallow him. He speeds forward. He is riding a wave at Jaws.

The surfer bolts down the
towering the wave. The wave behind
him stands 70 feet (21 meters) high.
He races ahead of its roaring crest.

Wave crest

BLAZER FACT

Extreme waves at
Jaws near Maui,
Hawaii, happen only
a few times each year.

Wave base

The wave begins to crash around the surfer. He speeds toward the base of the wave. The ride is over in less than 30 seconds. He has survived Jaws.

Surfboards

Surfers use two kinds of boards
to perform moves. Shortboards have
a pointed nose and sharp edges.
Longboards are heavy and straight.

Shortboard

Most surfers wear ankle leashes.
These straps keep surfers hooked to
their boards. Surfers wax their boards
to keep from slipping off.

Ankle leash

BLAZER FACT

In Hawaii, kids can compete on high school surf teams.

Longboard

Fin

Most shortboards have three fins on the bottom. Fins help surfers control their boards. Fins also help surfers twist and turn on the waves.

Surfboarding Diagram

Wave face

Nose

Deck

Wave crest

Ankle leash

Tricks

Surfers use a wave's speed and height to do aerials and grabs. They bounce off the wave and sail through the air.

Surfers need balance to perform
longboard tricks. They walk across
the deck. To hang 10, surfers ride
with their toes hanging over the nose.

Hang 10

Aerial
grab

Shortboarders use waves to do aerial moves. They pop off the wave's lip and grab their boards in the air. They flip backward to do a rail grab.

Rail grab

safety

Wipeouts are part of extreme surfing. Surfers know how to fall safely. They protect their heads with their hands and arms.

Surfers are good swimmers. Monster waves can trap surfers under the water. Surfers relax and let the water push them to the top.

BLAZER FACT

Surfers get "axed" by a wave when they are hit by its lip.

Glossary

aerial (AIR-ee-uhl)—a trick performed in the air

base (BAYSS)—the bottom of a wave

crest (KREST)—the top of a wave

fin (FIN)—a piece of wood or plastic on the underside of a surfboard

lip (LIP)—the tip of a wave that curls or plunges down

longboard (LAWNG-bord)—a surfboard that is about 9 feet (2.7 meters) long

rail (RAYL)—the side of a surfboard

shortboard (SHORT-bord)—a surfboard that is about 6 feet (1.8 meters) long

wipeout (WIPE-out)—a fall or crash

Read More

Crossingham, John, and Bobbie Kalman. *Extreme Surfing.* Extreme Sports No Limits! New York: Crabtree, 2004.

Herran, Joe, and Ron Thomas. *Surfing.* Action Sports. Philadelphia: Chelsea House, 2004.

Woods, Bob. *Water Sports.* Extreme Sports. Milwaukee: Gareth Stevens, 2004.

Internet Sites

FactHound offers a safe, fun way to find Internet sites related to this book. All of the sites on FactHound have been researched by our staff.

Here's how:

1. Visit *www.facthound.com*
2. Type in this special code **0736837868** for age-appropriate sites. Or enter a search word related to this book for a more general search.
3. Click on the **Fetch It** button.

FactHound will fetch the best sites for you!

Index